Creative Mandalas 1

Mandala Coloring Books Vol.1

Karim Benyagoub

Copyright © 2015 Karim Benyagoub

ISBN-10: 1508704066

ISBN-13: 978-1508704065

www.ingramcontent.com/pod-product-compliance
Lightning Source LLC
Chambersburg PA
CBHW080339290526

45790CB00010B/3759